D1643611

The
RESILIENCE
BOOK

A Helen Exley
QUOTATION COLLECTION

ILLUSTRATED BY JULIETTE CLARKE
EDITED BY HELEN EXLEY

Published in 2020 by Helen Exley® LONDON in Great Britain.
Illustrated by Juliette Clarke ©Helen Exley Creative Ltd 2020.
Design and creation by Helen Exley © Helen Exley Creative Ltd 2020.
All the words by Pam Brown, Dalton Exley, Charlotte Gray,
Pamela Dugdale, Helen M. Exley and Stuart & Linda
Macfarlane are © Helen Exley Creative Ltd 2020.

ISBN 978-1-78485-141-5

12 11   10 9 8 7 6 5 4 3 2 1

OTHER BOOKS IN THE SERIES

THE BOOK OF POSITIVE THOUGHTS   FOREVER TOGETHER

CALM AND MINDFULNESS   BELIEVE IN YOURSELF

MIX
Paper from
responsible sources
FSC® C081635
www.fsc.org

Helen Exley® LONDON
16 Chalk Hill, Watford, Hertfordshire, WD19 4BG, UK
www.helenexley.com

The
RESILIENCE
BOOK

A Helen Exley
QUOTATION COLLECTION

Resilience
is the ability to
find the inner strength
to bounce back from
a set-back or
challenge.

Resilience – is the ability to work
with adversity in such a way
that one comes through it unharmed
or even better for the experience.
Resilience means facing life's
difficulties with courage and patience –
refusing to give up.
It is the quality of character
that allows
a person or group of people
to rebound from misfortune, hardships
and traumas.

AUTHOR UNKNOWN

The way our culture is defining courage is so ridiculous. Courage has become Raiders of the Lost Ark, or riding in spaceships, killing people, taking enormous physical risks. To me, the kind of courage that's really interesting is someone whose spouse has Alzheimer's and yet manages to wake up every morning and be cheerful with that person and respectful of that person and find things to enjoy even though their day is very, very difficult. That kind of courage is really undervalued in our culture.

MARY PIPHER, B. 1947

The fact that courage
is expected of you
in the face of
the unbearable
gives you strength
for the rest of your life.

NELSON ROLIHLAHLA MANDELA (1918-2013)

The task ahead of us is never
as great as the power behind us.

ALCOHOLICS ANONYMOUS

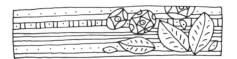

Someone was hurt before you,

wronged before you,

hungry before you,

frightened before you,

beaten before you,

humiliated before you,

raped before you...

Yet, someone survived...

You can do anything

you choose to do.

MAYA ANGELOU (1928-2014)

…when people confront situations…
in which there is no alternative,
they are usually very brave. It's like
we have hidden resources of strength
that we never use; we don't even know
that we have them, because we don't
need them. It's just sort of an immunity
of the system that is never challenged,
and when it is challenged,
our inner resources emerge.
In terrible moments, in moments
of revolution, of war or repression,
of illness or death,
people react with incredible strength.

ISABEL ALLENDE, B. 1942

Ever tried.
Ever failed.
No matter.
Try again.
Fail again.
Fail better.

SAMUEL BECKETT (1906-1989)

In order to succeed,
people need a sense of self-efficacy,
to struggle together with resilience
to meet the inevitable obstacles
and inequities of life.

ALBERT BANDURA, B. 1925

urance

Beyond talent
lie all the usual words:
discipline, love, luck –
but, most of all,
endurance.

JAMES BALDWIN (1924-1987)

I've learned from all my failures –
not all, but most of my learning
has come from my failures.
I don't know if you learn much from
success or happiness.
They are very nice, but coping –
really coping, so that you deal with
what is instead of what you'd like to be,
with the loss of ego
due to a profound failure or a loss
of love – strengthens you.

ELLEN BURSTYN, B. 1932

*The unendurable
is the beginning of
the curve of joy.*

DJUNA BARNES (1892-1982)

Do not allow your heart
to be obsessed by past sadness.
Hold to the joys, however small.
They are the catalyst that transforms
even the darkest sorrows
into the light of new beginnings.

PAM BROWN (1928-2014)

Never flinch, never weary, never despair.

SIR WINSTON CHURCHILL (1874-1965)

My scars remind me that I did indeed
survive my deepest wounds.
That in itself is an accomplishment.
And they bring to mind something else, too.
They remind me that the damage
life has inflicted on me has,
in many places, left me stronger
and more resilient.
What hurt me in the past has actually
made me better equipped to face
the present.

STEVE GOODIER, B. 1962

Completely exhausted, weary, massively outnumbered and outgunned. Is this the time to give up hope? No, it's exactly the time not to. It fascinates me how often hope has led, against all the odds, to incredible victories snatched right from the jaws of defeat. We can take this as inspiration for the struggles we face in our own lives. Never, ever give up.

DALTON EXLEY

I bend, but I

do not break.

Success seems to be largely a matter of
hanging on after others have let go.

I find hope
in the darkest of days,
and focus
in the brightest.

THE DALAI LAMA, B. 1935

Resilience isn't a single skill.
It's a variety of skills
and coping mechanisms.
To bounce back from bumps
in the road as well as failures,
you should focus on emphasizing
the positive.

JEAN CHATZKY, B. 1964

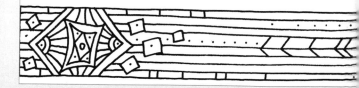

If you've been knocked down,
get up!
If you're feeling hurt or rejected,
get up!
If you've been floored
by emotional upheaval,
get up!
The reason I say
"get up!"
is because only by getting up can
someone move forward in life.

CYNTHIA COOPER

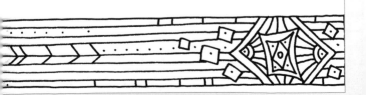

*The only way
to remove obstacles
is to face them head-on,
just like the buffalo
stands facing the wind.*

GOLDIE HAWN, B. 1945

I understand what it's like to have
to make changes to the pathway
you thought you were on,
taking tiny steps and having patience,
and having to work really hard
on your self-belief when you lose
confidence in your ability.
I did it every day, I know how easy
it can be to talk yourself out of something
before you actually get started.
But I also know how to dig deep,
summon that willpower
and find the guts and determination
to break through the barriers.

DAME KELLY HOLMES, B. 1970

We may encounter many defeats,
but we must not be defeated.

MAYA ANGELOU (1928-2014)

Faint not – fight on!
Tomorrow comes the song.

MALTBIE BABCOCK (1858-1901)

Life is

Life is a sorrow,
overcome it
Life is a song,
sing it.
Life is a struggle,
accept it.
Life is a tragedy,
confront it.
Life is an adventure,
dare it.
Life is luck,
make it.
Life is too precious,
do not destroy it.
Life is life,
fight for it.

MOTHER TERESA (1910-1997)

For my own emotional well-being I had to banish negativity from my mind. Lindbergh made it across the Atlantic; Houdini got out of those straitjackets; with enough money and grass-roots support, why shouldn't I be able to get out of this wheelchair? When you're trapped in a dark room, you think: Where's the exit? You find the exit by remaining calm and slowly feeling your way in the dark until you reach the door.

CHRISTOPHER REEVE (1952-2004)

For people sometimes believed
that it was safer to live with complaints,
was necessary to cooperate with grief,
was all right to become an accomplice
in self-ambush…
Take heart to flat out decide
to be well and stride into the future
sane and whole.

TONI CADE BAMBARA (1939-1995)

Adversity may seem a barren
and dismal land; but from it grows
strength of character,
from it flowers determination.
From adversity blossoms the people
with the wisdom and courage
to change the world.

STUART & LINDA MACFARLANE

You can't fail if

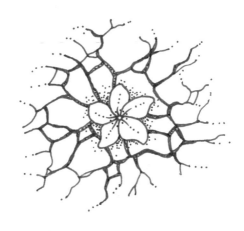

ou try.

BARONESS TANNI GREY-THOMPSON, B. 1969

Square your shoulders to the world,
be not the kind to quit;
It's not the load that weighs you down
but the way you carry it.

PROMISE MABELA

Courage doesn't always roar. Sometimes courage is the quiet voice at the end of the day that says "I will try again tomorrow."

MARY ANNE RADMACHER

Failure is not a stop sign,
a juddering halt.
It is simply the end of one particular road.
You have learned a lot.
Time to take that knowledge
and take another road.
Wiser and more courageous than before.

PAMELA DUGDALE

When a person trains once,
nothing happens.
When a person forces himself to do a thing
a hundred or a thousand times,
then he certainly has developed
in more ways than physical.
Is it raining?
That doesn't matter. Am I tired?
That doesn't matter either.
Then willpower will be no problem.

EMIL ZATNOPEK (1922-2000)

Every bump

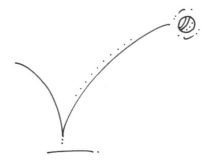

s a bounce.

ROBERT KRAFT

The best way to succeed is to double your failure rate.

THOMAS J. WATSON JR.

...everyone who wishes to gain true knowledge must climb the Hill Difficulty alone, and since there is no royal road to the summit, I must zigzag it in my own way. I slip back many times, I fall, I stand still, I run against the edge of hidden obstacles, I lose my temper and find it again and keep it better. I trudge on, I gain a little, I feel encouraged, I get more eager and climb higher and begin to see the widening horizon. Every struggle is a victory. One more effort and I reach the luminous cloud, the blue depths of the sky, the uplands of my desire.

HELEN KELLER (BORN BOTH DEAF AND BLIND) (1880-1968)

When you want to succeed in life
and achieve your objectives
you have to take risks.
Sometimes you'll fail and that's
part of learning to succeed.
But sometimes you can turn
a losing situation into a win
by having the determination,
the courage,
the fighting spirit
to make it happen, to win.

BILL CULLEN, B. 1942

Courage is finding the inner strength and bravery required when confronting danger, difficulty or opposition. Courage is the energy current behind all great actions and the spark that ignites the initial baby steps of growth. It resides deep within each of us, ready to be accessed in those moments when you need to forge ahead or break through seemingly insurmountable barriers. It is the intangible force that propels you forward on your journey.

CHERIE CARTER-SCOTT, B. 1949

If there is no

wind, row.

LATIN PROVERB

*Obstacles
in the pathway of
the weak
become stepping stones
in the pathway
of the strong.*

THOMAS CARLYLE (1795-1881)

What matters
is not the size of the dog
in the fight,
but the size of the fight
in the dog.

DWIGHT D. EISENHOWER (1890-1969)

Just as thousands before
have mastered adversities
so can we.
Troubles can bring out the best in us
and strengthen us
as we overcome them.

DALTON EXLEY

If life teaches us anything,

it's maybe that it's necessary

to suffer some defeats.

Look at a diamond:

It is the result of extreme pressure.

Less pressure, it is a crystal;

less than that, it's coal;

and less than that, it is fossilized leaves

or just plain dirt.

MAYA ANGELOU (1928-2014)

There is probably not a single man
or woman, who, mostly from self-interest,
it is true, but it might also have been
from a superior motive,
has not overcome powerful obstacles
and accomplished things
extremely difficult to undertake.

ERNEST DIMNET (1866 -1954)

COU

The power to hold on in spite of everything, the power to endure – this is the winner's quality. Persistence is the ability to face defeat again and again without giving up – to push on in the face of great difficulty, knowing that victory can be yours. Persistence means taking pains to overcome every obstacle, and to do what's necessary to reach your goals.

WYNN DAVIS

*Often the test of courage
is not to die but to live.*

COUNT VITTORIO ALFIERI (1749-1803)

Resilience is accepting
your new reality,
even if it's less good than the one
you had before.
You can fight it,
you can do nothing but
scream about what you've lost,
or you can accept that
and try to put together
something that's good.

ELIZABETH EDWARDS

A moment of courage in the heat
of battle is courage enough –
but the long-enduring courage
of the man or woman, or the child,
who, victims of persecution or
catastrophe, struggle to hold
their family together,
to find food and shelter,
to hold out hope when hope is gone.
These are the true,
unlauded, heroes and heroines...

PAM BROWN (1928-2014)

You may write me down in history
With your bitter, twisted lies,
You may trod me in the very dirt
But still, like dust, I'll rise.

Just like moons and like suns,
With the certainty of tides,
Just like hopes springing high,
Still I'll rise.

MAYA ANGELOU (1928-2014)

I'll rise.

Develop success from failures.
Discouragement and failure
are two of the surest
stepping stones to success.

DALE CARNEGIE (1888-1955)

You do not determine
a person's greatness
by their talent or wealth,
as the world does,
but rather by what it takes
to discourage them.

JERRY FALWELL

Don't stop because you're tired.
Keep going because you're almost there.

RITU GHATOUREY

If you suffer setbacks or disappointments,
you should pick yourself up,
focus on new goals and try again.
It doesn't matter where you end up
as long as you are trying.

BARONESS TANNI GREY-THOMPSON, B. 1969

Our greatest glory is not in never falling, but in rising every time we fall.

CONFUCIUS (551 B.C.-479 B.C.)

What really counts in life
is the quiet meeting of every difficulty
with the determination to get out of it
all the good there is.

HELEN KELLER (BORN BOTH DEAF AND BLIND) (1880-1968)

We have a saying: "The lotus grows in the mud."… The lotus is the most beautiful flower, whose petals open one by one. But it will only grow in mud. In order to grow and gain wisdom, first you must have the mud – the obstacles of life and its suffering… The mud speaks of the common ground that we humans share, no matter what our stations in life… Whether we have it all or we have nothing, we are all faced with the same obstacles: sadness, loss, illness, dying and death. If we are to strive as human beings to gain more wisdom, more kindness and more compassion, we must have the intention to grow as a lotus and open each petal one by one.

KUTENLA, BUDDHIST MONK

Every problem has a gi

We think sometimes when things
don't go the right way, when we suffer a defeat,
that all has ended. Not true.
It is only a beginning, always. Greatness comes
not when things always go good for you,
but the greatness comes when you are
really tested, when you take some knocks,
some disappointments, when sadness comes.
Because only if you have been in the deepest
valley can you ever know how magnificent
it is to be on the highest mountain.

RICHARD NIXON (1913-1994)

r you in its hands.

RICHARD BACH, B. 1936

What does not destroy me,
makes me strong.

FRIEDRICH WILHELM NIETZSCHE (1844-1900)

*The difference
in winning
and losing
is most often...
not quitting.*

WALT DISNEY (1901-1966)

…family and friends aren't always
ready to make the journey when you are,
and you just have to keep plowing along
whether they have confidence in you or not.
That can be very lonely.
The challenge, whenever you create
anything, is to persevere and push away
the negative voices.
And the more you accomplish,
the louder they get.
The key is to shut them off and to trust
in your heart where you're going.

ANNE BANCROFT

Strength

We ought to remember that we are not the only ones to find ourselves at an apparent impasse. Just as a kite rises against the wind, even the worst of troubles can strengthen us. As thousands before us have met the identical fate and mastered it, so can we!

DR. R. BRASCH

It's easy to give up when things are hard but I believe we have to keep chasing our dreams and our goals... And once we decide to do something, we should never look back, never regret it.

SIR RICHARD BRANSON, B. 1950

...out of every adversity

omes opportunity.

RACHEL ELNAUGH

No one at the outset can expect to hit
the bullseye – or even the target itself
sometimes. But that is no failure. It does not
diminish the attempt and indeed helps
to hone the skill, so that later shots will fly
more surely to their mark.

STEPHEN BOWKETT

If we, passing in the train,
could lift the roofs we pass,
the houses in their rows,
the uniformity,
we would find a thousand stories
of love and kindness,
trouble and endurance.
Courage beyond belief.

PAM BROWN (1928-2014)

With ordinary talent
and extraordinary perseverance,
all things are attainable.

THOMAS FOWELL BUXTON (1786-1845)

We have always got more strength than we realise. All of us.

HELEN M. EXLEY

Ordinary life evokes more extraordinary courage than combat or adventure because both the chances and inevitabilities of life – grief, illness, disappointment, pain, struggle, poverty, loss, terror, heartache: all of them common features of the human condition, and all of them experienced by hundreds of thousands of people every day – demand kinds of endurance and bravery that make clambering up Everest seem an easier alternative.

A. C. GRAYLING, B. 1949

Resilience is all about
being able to overcome the unexpected.
Sustainability is about survival.
The goal of resilience is to thrive.

JAMAIS CASCIO, B. 1966

The gem cannot be polished without friction,
nor the person perfected without trials.

CHINESE PROVERB

People who do great deeds
such as climbing Everest
or travelling to the South Pole
are often described as courageous.
But what they do is out of choice
so is it true courage?
Perhaps the real heroes are
the young children who beg
in the streets or scavenge
on dumps to earn a few coins
so they can feed siblings.
That takes real courage,
real love and real hope.

STUART & LINDA MACFARLANE

Great acts of courage
are acclaimed all through history.
Yet the quiet endurance
and resilience of unknown
men and women
has kept our species alive.

CHARLOTTE GRAY

Storms make oaks take deeper root.

GEORGE HERBERT (1593-1633)

The nature of pines and cypresses
cannot be found until
the freezing winter comes;
the character of a superior person
cannot be seen until great difficulties
come upon you.

CHINESE SAYING

Be free. Head high. Be determined and strong.

PAM BROWN (1928-2014)

Within a system which denies
the existence of basic
human rights, fear tends to be
the order of the day.
Yet even under the most crushing
state machinery,
courage rises up again and again.

AUNG SAN SUU KYI, B. 1945

Never give in,
never give in,
never; never; never; never –
in nothing, great or small,
large or petty – never give in
except to convictions of honour
and good sense.
Never yield to force.
Never yield to the apparently
overwhelming might of the enemy.

SIR WINSTON CHURCHILL (1874-1965)

*I have discovered
the secret that
after climbing a great hill,
one only finds
that there are many more
hills to climb.*

NELSON ROLIHLAHLA MANDELA (1918-2013)

Each one of us has an inner strength,

a capacity for survival.

No life is without some element of grief

and pain. Keep faith in yourself

during difficult times –

your inner strength

will see you through.

STUART & LINDA MACFARLANE

Perseverance is failing
nineteen times
and succeeding the twentieth.

JULIE ANDREWS, B. 1935

When things reach their limit, they are forced to bounce back.

CHINESE PROVERB

It is courage that restores hope to the heart.
In our day to day lives, we often show
courage without realizing it.
However, it is only when we are afraid
that courage becomes a question.
Courage is amazing because it can tap
in to the heart of fear, taking that frightened
energy and turning it towards initiative,
creativity, action and hope.
When courage comes alive, imprisoning
walls become frontiers of new possibilities,
difficulty becomes invitation
and the heart comes into a new rhythm
of trust and sureness.

JOHN O'DONOHUE (1956-2008)

There is glory in

Yⁱ ou must make a decision
that you are going to move on.
It won't happen automatically.
You will have to rise up and say,
"I don't care how hard this is,
I don't care how disappointed I am,
I'm not going to let this get the best of me.
I'm moving on with my life."

JOEL OSTEEN, B. 1963

I don't measure a person's success
by how high he climbs
but how high he bounces
when he hits bottom.

GENERAL GEORGE S. PATTON (1885-1945)

great mistake.

NATHALIA CRANE (1913-1998)

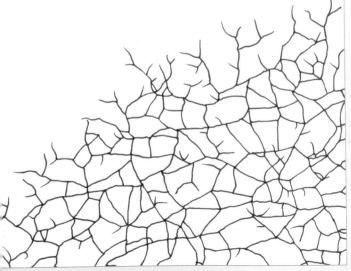

The
bamboo
that
bends
is
stronger
than
the
oak
that
resists.

JAPANESE PROVERB

Jump into the middle of things, get your hands dirty, fall flat on your face, and then reach for the stars.

JOAN L. CURCIO

Only as high as I reach can I grow,

Only as far as I seek can I go,

Only as deep as I look can I see,

Only as much as I dream can I be.

KAREN RAVN

At some time, often when we least expect it, we all have to face overwhelming challenges. We are more troubled than we have ever been before; we may doubt that we have what it takes to endure.
It is very tempting to give up, yet we have to find the will to keep going.
But even when we discover what motivates us, we realise that we can't go the distance alone...
Hope must be as real, and built on the same solid foundation, as a lighthouse;

in that way it is different from optimism
or wishful thinking.
When we have hope, we discover powers
within ourselves we may have never known –
the power to make sacrifices,
to endure, to heal, and to love.
Once we choose hope,
everything is possible.
We are all on this sea together.
But the lighthouse is always there,
ready to show us the way home.

CHRISTOPHER REEVE (1952-2004)

*We are all
in the gutter,
but some of us
are looking
at the stars.*

OSCAR WILDE (1854-1900)

Again and again,
the impossible problem is solved
when we see that the problem is only
a tough decision waiting to be made.

DR. ROBERT SCHULLER (1926-2015)

True grit
is making a decision
and standing by it,
doing what must be done.

JOHN WAYNE (1907-1979)

When you go through hardships and decide
not to surrender, that is strength.

ARNOLD SCHWARZENEGGER, B. 1947

All of us experience fear,
but when we confront
and acknowledge it,
we are able to turn it
into courage.
Being courageous
does not mean never
being scared;
it means acting as you know
you must even though you
are undeniably afraid.

ARCHBISHOP DESMOND TUTU, B. 1931

I have met brave women
who are exploring the outer edge of
human possibility, with no history
to guide them, and with a courage
to make themselves vulnerable
that I find moving beyond the words
to express it.

GLORIA STEINEM, B. 1934

$\triangleright \cdots \triangleright \, \triangleright \, \triangleright \cdots \triangleright \, \triangleright \cdots$

Many of you
Have seen tears
And disappointments.
You regret that which was.
You gaze upon your mistakes
And carry your guilt.
But
Were they mistakes?
Or
Did you make them
That you may learn?

CLEARWATER

...despair is going to make you weaker,
it's not going to change one fact.
The battle is to try to jack up whatever
is positive. I hadn't been killed, I wasn't
being tortured and the food was OK...
There are people who have been told
they have nine months to live and most of
those people handle that with grace.
I told myself that I was waiting to live my life
again and it would be shameful if I couldn't
do it with dignity. You've got to keep
the waves of depression and anxiety and fear
at a minimum. I just lived through the day.
Just keep living, thinking things are going
to get better, the sun is going to come out.
It always does. And it did.

ALAN JOHNSTON, B. 1962

It isn't for the moment you are struck that you need courage, but for the long uphill climb back to sanity and faith and security.

ANNE MORROW LINDBERGH (1906-2001)

When you get to the end
of all the light you know
And it's time to step into
the darkness of the unknown
Faith is knowing that one of two things
shall happen
Either you will be given something solid
to stand on
Or you will be taught how to fly.

EDWARD TELLER (1908-2003)

*The oak fought the wind
and was broken,
the willow bent
when it must and survived.*

ROBERT JORDAN (1948-2007)

At the core of life is a hard purposefulness,
a determination to live.

HOWARD THURMAN

Tough times never last, but tough people do.

DR. ROBERT SCHULLER (1926-2015)

If you have made mistakes...
there is always another chance for you...
you may have a fresh start
any moment you choose,
for this thing we call "failure"
is not the falling down,
but the staying down.

MARY PICKFORD (1893-1979)

"This too will pass." I was taught these words by my grandmother as a phrase that is to be used at all times in your life. When things are spectacularly dreadful; when things are absolutely appalling; when everything is superb and wonderful and marvellous and happy – say these four words to yourself. They will give you a sense of perspective and help you also to make the most of what is good and be stoical about what is bad.

CLAIRE RAYNER (1931-2010)

${P}$eople won't forget,
but they're going to say, "Great.
After his downfall, the guy
took care of his problems and won again."
That will be the biggest thrill of my life.

BEN JOHNSON, B. 1961

I still want to do my work,
I still want to do my livingness.
And I have lived.
I have been fulfilled.
I recognized what I had,
and I never sold it short.
And I ain't through yet!

LOUISE NEVELSON (1900-1988)

Life shrinks or expands
in proportion to one's courage.

ANAÏS NIN (1903-1977)

The world is round and the place
which may seem like the end may also
be the beginning.

IVY BAKER PRIEST (1905-1975)

*T*he harder you fall,
the higher you bounce.

DOUG HORTON

I'm grateful for all my problems.
As each of them was overcome
I became stronger and more able
to meet those yet to come.
I grew on my difficulties.

J. C. PENNEY (1875-1971)

Don't ever make the mistake of thinking that losing is the same as failing, or that losing means terminal derailment. This is rarely, if ever, the case. Winning and losing are one-dimensional judgements that are made easily when you are sitting as a spectator in the stands. Losing once

does not mean that you haven't enough talent to succeed in future – it is simply an opportunity to learn, to expand understanding of the task and develop self-knowledge and to find out what improvements have to be made in order to win next time.

LORD SEBASTIAN COE, B. 1956

If you first
don't succeed,
Try,
try again.

WILLIAM EDWARD HICKSON (1803-1870)

Resilience is very different
than being numb.
Resilience means you experience,
you feel,
you fail,
you hurt.
You fall.
But, you keep going.

YASMIN MOGAHED, B. 1980

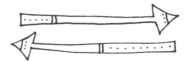

again

What separates the winners
from the losers is that winners
are able to handle problems
and crises that they never
imagined would occur.
You hit the floor,
but what counts is how fast
you can get up and regroup.

GEORGETTE MOSBACHER, B. 1947

*When your house
has quite disappeared,
you mustn't complain.
You still have all that snow
to do with what you like.*

FROM "EEYORE'S GLOOMY LITTLE INSTRUCTION BOOK"

My will shall shape my future.
Whether I fail or succeed shall be
no one's doing but my own.
I am the force; I can clear any obstacle
before me or I can be lost in the maze.
My choice; my responsibility;
win or lose,
only I hold the key to my destiny.

ELAINE MAXWELL

When you get into a tight place
and everything goes against you,
till it seems as though
you could not hang on
a minute longer,
never give up then,
for that is just the place
and time that the tide will turn.

HARRIET BEECHER STOWE (1811-1896)

You never know how strong you are
until being strong is the only choice you have.

BOB MARLEY (1945-1981)

It is in times of greatest difficulty
that you discover your greatest strengths.

STUART & LINDA MACFARLANE

It's not whether you get knocked down.
It's whether you get up again.

VINCE LOMBARDI (1913-1970)

Great works are performed not by strength
but by perseverance.

DR. SAMUEL JOHNSON (1709-1784)

Every exit is an entry somewhere else.

TOM STOPPARD, B. 1937

Some minds seem almost to create themselves,
springing up under every disadvantage
and working their solitary but irresistible way
through a thousand obstacles.

WASHINGTON IRVING (1783-1859)

Be like the bird that, passing on her flight
awhile on boughs too slight,
feels them give way beneath her, and yet sings,
knowing that she hath wings.

VICTOR HUGO (1802-1885)

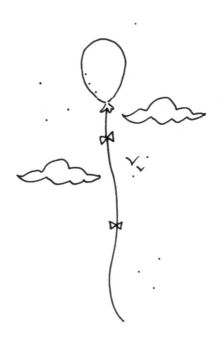

*You're braver
than you believe,
and stronger
than you seem,
and smarter
than you think.*

A. A. MILNE (1882-1956)

We don't develop courage
by being happy every day.
We develop it by surviving difficult
times and challenging adversity.

BARBARA DE ANGELIS, B. 1951

However hard the knock or however hard
the path is that you have to follow,
there is ultimately some good,
something you have to learn through it.

DAME JUDI DENCH, B. 1934

Life begins at the en

I didn't have anybody, really,
no foundation in life,
so I had to make my own way.
Always. From the start.
I had to go out in the world
and become strong…

TINA TURNER, B. 1939

f your comfort zone.

NEALE DONALD WALSCH

The miracle, or the power, that elevates
the few is to be found in their industry,
application, and perseverance
under the prompting of a brave,
determined spirit.

MARK TWAIN (1835-1910)

If one window closes,
run to the next window –
or break down a door.

BROOKE SHIELDS, B. 1965

Master yourself,
and become king of the world around you.
Let no odds, chastisement,
exile, doubt, fear, or ANY mental virii
prevent you from accomplishing your dreams.
Never be a victim of life;
be its conqueror.

MIKE NORTON

What shall we do
when hope is gone?
The words leapt
like a leaping sword:
Sail on!
Sail on!
Sail on!
and on!

JOAQUIN MILLER (1839-1913)

*Our greatest weakness
lies in giving up.
The most certain way
to succeed
is always to try
just one more time.*

THOMAS EDISON (1847-1931)

Character consists of what you do
on the third and fourth tries.

JAMES A. MICHENER (1907-1997)

There's a lot of stress out there, and to handle it, you just need to believe in yourself; always go back to the person that you know you are, and don't let anybody tell you any different, because everyone's special and everyone's awesome.

MCKAYLA MARONEY, B. 1995

Challenges are what make life interesting; overcoming them is what makes life meaningful.

JOSHUA J. MARINE

It is not the critic who counts; not the man who points out how the strong man stumbles, or where the doer of deeds could have done them better. The credit belongs to the man who is actually in the arena, whose face is marred by dust and sweat and blood; who strives valiantly; who errs, and comes short again and again; because there is not effort without error and shortcoming; but who does actually

strive to do the deeds; who knows the great

enthusiasms, the great devotions; who spends

himself in a worthy cause, who at the best knows

in the end the triumphs of high achievement

and who at the worst, if he fails, at least fails

while daring greatly, so that his place shall

never be with those cold and timid souls

who know neither victory nor defeat.

THEODORE ROOSEVELT (1858-1919)

Birds sing after a storm,
why shouldn't people feel as free
to delight in whatever remains to them?

ROSE FITZGERALD KENNEDY (1890-1995)

The lowest ebb is the turn of the tide.

VINCE LOMBARDI (1913-1970)

If at night you can look at yourself and say,
"I faced my problems and did not turn away"
you have conquered the day.

STUART & LINDA MACFARLANE

I am not a has-been. I'm a will be.

LAUREN BACALL (1924-2014)

The Cherokee learned long ago to say, "We no longer fall down when something challenges us. We no longer see ourselves as victims. But we are strong and able to overcome the most severe critic and break every habit that has kept us bound."

JOYCE SEQUICHE HIFLER

If you fall behind, run faster. Never give up, never surrender, and rise up against the odds.

JESSE JACKSON, B. 1941

Courage is going
from failure to failure
without losing enthusiasm.

SIR WINSTON CHURCHILL (1874-1965)

Success is...  a serie

We must always take failure not as a finished product or as the culmination of an experience but, rather, as part of the process of experience.

SRI CHINMOY (1931-2007)

First ask yourself: What is the worst that can happen? Then prepare to accept it. Then proceed to improve on the worst.

DALE CARNEGIE (1888-1955)

f glorious defeats...

MAHATMA GANDHI (1869-1948)

I wanted you to see what real courage is, instead of getting the idea that courage is a man with a gun in his hand. It's when you know you're licked before you begin but you begin anyway and you see it through no matter what.

HARPER LEE (1926-2016)

We are not a product of what has happened to us in our past. We have the power of choice.

STEPHEN R. COVEY (1932-2012)

No successful entrepreneur
has got where they are without
a considerable number of failures.
It's what they learn from;
in fact you could argue that if you
are not failing you are not
trying hard enough!

RICHARD PARKES CORDOCK

Just because you fall off a horse, you don't have to lie there. If all you can do is crawl, then crawl. If you can get up, walk. If you have to limp, find something to lean on and keep going. Never say, "This is it," and give up.

BEAR HEART (MUSKOGEE) (1918-2008)

Strength shows, not only in the ability
to persist, but the ability to start over.

F. SCOTT FITZGERALD (1896-1940)

No matter what happens to you,
you don't need to give up on life.
You can achieve whatever you want to
if you put your mind to it.

PRINCE HARRY, B. 1984

To lie sleepless with pain at night.
or to wake every morning and feel
the return of grief,
yet to get up and carry on as best you can,
is courage itself.

A. C. GRAYLING, B. 1949

We don't make mistakes.
We just have learnings.

ANNE WILSON SCHAEF

Failing is not a crime.
What is important is that if you fail
you have the energy and the will
to pull yourself up and keep going.

WANGARI MAATHAI (1940-2011)

Don't give up. Keep going.
There is always a chance that you
will stumble onto something terrific.
I have never heard of anyone stumbling
over anything while sitting down.

ANN LANDERS

Character cannot be developed
in ease and quiet.
Only through experience of trial
and suffering can we be strengthened,
vision cleared, ambition inspired,
and success achieved.

HELEN KELLER (BORN BOTH DEAF AND BLIND) (1880-1968)

When one door shuts another opens.

SAMUEL PALMER (1805-1881)

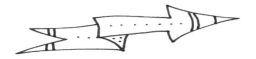

Many people lose heart and give up
when success doesn't happen
when they want it to, but that is the crucial time.
That is the point when focus, determination,
persistence and belief, needs to be at its
strongest because that is the period in
which you will discover your "alter ego".
That is the person inside of you that is
so committed to achieving your goal
that you will become like the strongest
of laser beams, capable of blowing away
any obstacle that stands in your way.

PETER EBDON, B. 1970

Courage is not having
the strength to go on.
It is going on when
you don't have the strength.

THEODORE ROOSEVELT (1858-1919)

Things don't go wrong
and break your heart so you can become
bitter and give up.
They happen to break you down
and build you up so you
can be all you were intended to be.

CHARLES JONES

Einstein's three rules of work:

1) Out of clutter find simplicity.
2) From discord make harmony.
3) In the middle of difficulty lies opportunity.

ALBERT EINSTEIN (1879-1955)

The dry desert landscape can burst into bloom after the thunderstorm.

SUSAN SQUELLATI FLORENCE

One's doing well if age improves
even slightly one's capacity to hold
on to that vital truism:
"This too shall pass."

ALAIN DE BOTTON, B. 1969

I honour you for every time this year you:
got back up vibrated higher
shined your light and loved and elevated
beyond – the call of duty.

LALAH DELIA

Heroism is the brilliant triumph over fear...
Heroism is the dazzling
and brilliant concentration of courage.

HENRI FRÉDÉRIC AMIEL (1821-1881)

Stubbornly persist, and you will find
that the limits of your stubbornness
go well beyond the stubbornness of your limits.

ROBERT BRAULT

*Things do not happen.
Things are made to
happen.*

PRESIDENT JOHN F. KENNEDY (1917-1963)

Whatever you do, do it with all your might.
Work at it, early and late,
in season and out of season,
not leaving a stone unturned,
and never deferring for one single hour
that which can be done just as well right now.

P. T. BARNUM (1810-1891)

I've missed more than
nine thousand shots in my career.
I've lost almost three hundred games.
Twenty-six times I've been trusted to
take the game-winning shot
and missed. I've failed over and over
and over again in my life.
And that is why I succeed.

MICHAEL JORDAN, B. 1963

Start where you are.
Use what you have.
Do what you can.

ARTHUR ASHE (1943-1993)

You gotta play the hand that's dealt you.
There may be pain in that hand, but you play it.

JAMES BRADY (1940-2014)

One's neighbour in a placid suburban street
may be far more courageous
than an acknowledged hero.
Loss, pain, disappointment, fear –
hidden under smiles
and cheerful conversation.

PAM BROWN (1928-2014)

I have known failures.
Those I have run from
taught me nothing.
Those I got to know intimately
permitted me quantum leaps
forward. The failures are
what deliver us to ourselves.
You don't get Real
by playing it safe.

JANE FONDA, B. 1937

Times of general calamity and confusion
have ever been productive of the greatest minds.
The purest ore is produced from
the hottest furnace, and the brightest thunderbolt
is elicited from the darkest storms.

CHARLES CALEB COLTON (1780-1832)

Fall seven time:

Soldiers may show great courage
– but have been trained to face attack.
They know the likelihood of injury or death
they face. They are prepared.
...Ordinary people are not.
Catastrophe, tragedy come with no warning –
And yet they face them with extraordinary
courage, enduring against all odds.
No medals. No commendations.
But the respect of all who know them.

PAM BROWN (1928-2014)

tand up eight.

JAPANESE PROVERB

Be grateful for all
the difficult situations in life
because you can learn something
from each one.

BEAR HEART (MUSKOGEE) (1918-2008)

The world breaks everyone,
and afterward many are strong
in the broken places.

ERNEST HEMINGWAY (1899-1961)

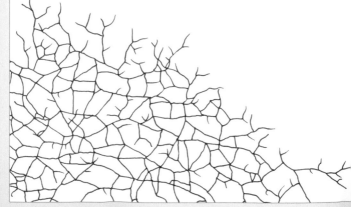

There exist some evils so terrible
and some misfortunes so horrible
that we dare not think of them,
whilst their very aspect makes us
shudder; but if they happen
to fall on us, we find ourselves
stronger than we imagined,
we grapple with our
ill luck, and behave better
than we expected we should.

JEAN DE LA BRUYÈRE (1645-1696)

*Ride on! Rough-shod
if need be, smooth-shod
if that will do,
but ride on! Ride on
over all obstacles,
and win the race!*

CHARLES DICKENS (1812-1870)

Perseverance is not a long race; it is many
short races one after another.

WALTER ELLIOTT

Strength does not come from physical capacity.
It comes from an indomitable will.

MAHATMA GANDHI (1869-1948)

The question is not whether
you're frightened or not,
but whether you or the fear is in control.
The correct thing to tell yourself is,
"If I do get frightened,
I will stay in command."

DR. HERBERT FENSTERHEIM

*Courage takes many forms.
There is physical courage,
there is moral courage.
Then there is a still higher
type of courage –
the courage to brave pain,
to live with it, to never
let others know of it
and to still find joy in life;
to wake up in the morning
with an enthusiasm
for the day ahead.*

HOWARD COSELL (1918-1995)